Expanding Horizons Through
Creative Expressions

# Expanding Horizons Through Creative Expressions:
## Reflections and Thoughts Related to the Struggle for Peace, Sustainability, Equality, and the Search for Humanity

Volume I

OBIORA EMBRY

# CONTENTS

*

**This is dedicated**

**to those that believed in me from the beginning and**

**knew I would do great things**

*

# PROLOGUE

02 May 2007

    This body of work is a compilation of my thoughts and ideas that began 10+ years ago...these musings are part of a larger and greater continuum that began before I was reborn and regained the *humanity* that I had lost. I have been restoring my humanity through the fostering of **peace**, *love*, understanding, a desire to restore the balance of ***Mother Earth***, and a search for the spiritual.

    The search for the spiritual was resurrected because it was put on the back burner when my focus shifted to material goods and wealth rather than my connection with the Earth—without *her*, we humans will perish as there is no other place in the Milky Way Galaxy we can inhabit. And even if we found another *home*, how long would it take for us to make that planet uninhabitable? 10 years? 30 years? 100 years?

    I believe that we need to develop the capacity to understand and heed the thoughts posed in the 1970s by the late James (Jimmy) Boggs

when he co-authored <u>Revolution and Evolution in the Twentieth Century</u>.
In the book, he stated the following:

> Human beings have been compelled to manifest their humanity in
> their technological capacity, to grow food, to make fires, to build
> dams, to invent lathes and computers. Simply to survive, we have
> concentrated our powers on producing things, evading critical
> questions of our relationships with one another and to Nature. As a
> result, we have become technologically overdeveloped and politically
> and socially underdeveloped. We will not regain our membership in
> the human race, until we recognize that our greatest need is not to
> develop the productive forces (which was a dominant concern of Karl
> Marx because he was creating his ideas in a period of material
> scarcity) but to struggle with one another and with ourselves to get rid
> of outmoded ideas and fears which keep us from grappling with the
> complex issues of our relationships with one another and with our
> natural environment[1].

1. Boggs, James and Grace Lee Boggs. *Revolution and Evolution in the Twentieth Century*. New York: Monthly Review Press, December 5,

1974. Print.


    This *struggle* that Jimmy Boggs discusses is a piece of the puzzle that we collectively lack but need to develop so we can create a better future with an emphasis on peace, expanding our horizons, and healing ourselves.

    Through my poetry (rhyming and non-rhyming), essays, and editorials, I try to make sense of the past and offer solutions for the present, so we can change the future for the better.

Sincerely,

*Obiora Embry*

# INTRODUCTION

"At the risk of seeming ridiculous, let me say that the true revolutionary is guided by a great feeling of love.  It is impossible to think of a genuine revolutionary lacking this quality."
— Ernesto "Che" Guevara

Peace and love, the only ways to a better life for you, me, and everyone.  We need to eliminate the *me vs. you* and *me vs. the world* mindsets and develop alternatives to the "industrialized" and "civilized" societies that Western thought and influence has created.  We need to develop a "world that works for all."

In seeking peace, there has to be an absence of violence as well as the ideologies of superiority and inferiority that create jealousy, animosity, and can lead to conflict and chaos.  If we are going to create la paz (peace) on Earth, then ALL weapons—hand-held, semi-/automatic, rifles and shotguns, chemical warfare, biological warfare, nuclear warfare, laser warfare, other weapons, etc.—need to be dismantled and destroyed, including those that are built and used every day by the U.S. *corporament* (corporations + government).

Threats and actions of violence only begets more violence, so, why do we feel that violence directed at others will lead to peace? If we think that violent actions can lead to peace, then we must be blind to the truth or cannot "see the forest for the trees."

We have to develop and create a better understanding of the world in which we live...we can no longer view our neighbors from a distance, or hope that the problems another nationality, sex, group, or country has is their problem and that it will eventually blow-over. "Everything is connected" and since this is the case, the United States cannot continue to justify its malicious, deceitful, hypocritical, and diabolical actions. Our individual and collective actions are not justified by our false sense of superiority nor the false assumption that we are innocent and never wrong.

There is a revolution brewing here and abroad that will be one of the greatest in human history but only, if we have "a small group of thoughtful, committed citizens" ready to create change. With this group, we can change our country and bring peace to the world by fostering love: a love for self, a love for family, a zest for peace, and a desire to see a "world that works for all."

# 1

## The Problem

**Untitled — 08-05-02**

The lies,
are stumbling blocks on the way to the truth,
keeping us blinded and unable to see reality.
No wonder some drugs are still illegal...
They can help those who use them
see beyond "The Matrix"
and see reality for what it really is.

Brainwashed,
since birth
the whole country is cursed
not realizing the trap door
beneath the floor
that keeps us running in place
never seeing life or reality face-to-face.

"You can't handle the truth!"
like the cat going on missions that are impossible.
Improbable cause before
truth detectors following the
statue of slavery,

which leads to bribery
of the truth,
which "A Few Good Men" couldn't handle.
Lies need to be dismantled
like a bike needing a new chain.

Tapped into the brain
off radio frequencies,
while EMF fields
bombard and disrupt the signal
broadcasted to unleash the truth.
You don't have to be a super sleuth
to know that you have been lied to
and that now it's time to seek the truth.

Say Bye, Bye to MK-ULTRA
and hello to the Deathstar,
which is far from our mind,
but constantly watching our every move
like a King on a chessboard.

There is no greater pain
than realizing that you have been
lied to your WHOLE life.
Couldn't face the lies,
now that I know the truth...
still stuck on stupid
because I can't see to break the mold
that keeps me trapped.

Left my 3rd 👁
when I was younger
because I couldn't understand its use,
but now I feel abused
and used.
Not sure who to trust
or what to trust.

They don't care
as long as their pockets get fatter.
The pursuit of money brought the downfall of many civilizations,
now it will bring the end of the world.
Funny (but tragic) how many people spend their lives
trying to collect something they can't use
or take with them when they die.

I wonder how many innocent people died
before you received your new ride
or your stock options
with the cash advance.
For every advance
in technology another 1,000 die.
When will we understand that
we are only bringing the world closer to death?
With every step
we take,
another species dies,
but we are too busy listening to the lies
to hear the whats and whys.

Ignorant to the facts

about our exploitation of the map,
trading arms covertly
with enemies and allies.
It's too bad
the people here can't see
the hypocrisies of a nation
that can't exist
in its present state
with the land treaties
protected by a Constitution,
few know
but many use
when it suits their purpose.

Bias to the facts
except when it's happening to you.
Too few could care
how many died last year
to produce the clothes you wear.

Triangular trade
that seems to evade
a whole nation
stuck in their ways.
It's a new form of slavery,
left the chains in the past
began the present with mass hypnosis.
Enslavement of the mind
because you have been brainwashed since birth.
Can't see freedom
for what it's worth,

but we have a thirst for freedom,
even though we tell the whole world
and ourselves that we already have it.

**Excerpt from <u>Times Done Changed</u>**

Minimum wage,
what is the minimum you can pay me
when I got three kids,
and a college education from one of the most expensive schools?
I still can't find a decent paying job,
one that helps to feed, clothe, and provide shelter for my
    children.
Who's to say the minimum is
enough in every city, every town, and county?
When will people see that something needs to be changed?
A national *living wage* is what's needed,
not a national minimum wage that has our youth
and many adults mad as hell,
preferring to slang or hustle than make chump change
that can't put food on anyone's table let alone clothes on their
    backs.
This society must have forgotten the times in which we live,
as more teenagers are becoming the head of their households
and/or have children they need to and should help to support.

As the forecasts predicted,
the rich are getting richer
and the poor are getting poorer,
lengthening the fine line walked
between the rich and poor.
Soon I wonder, will the rich even
care that I get paid less than his or her child
for doing the same job more efficiently and effectively?

## Untitled — 04-04-03

I only need one time
to blow your mind
and to unleash a chemical imbalance
that your heart couldn't manage
who's to blame for the damage
when the media makes people panic
and rip apart the streets
and their neighbors because they are intrigued by the beat
that gives them orders, so they don't have to think?
so the few are chastised
since we are not baptized
and are not overflowing with ignorance
it's sad when folks can learn all the new dances
but can't tell fact from fiction
they be fishin'
but for the wrong knowledge
usually preferring no knowledge
especially not of self
so the truth evades them like stealth
from the pollution, contamination, and disrespect
of the air, land, and water, which make up Mother Earth
we rob our seeds of their life before birth
but you know what's worse
you ain't feeling what I said
too used to getting beat in the head
with lies from the media and head
of state
who refuses all debates
'cause he knows then the world will know he's a fake,

a puppet,
a pawn,
yet we fail to see the wizard behind the curtain
which tells US for certain
this ain't only happening in Kansas or Oz.
we got people who have been playing US since the dawn
we are like the Muppets
without Henson

### Untitled — 04-24-03

Rhymes are lethal
like injection
or Ice Cube
hard to figure out like a Rubik Cube
plus you steppin' in the wrong direction
lookin' past the clues that show like an erection
in my pants
we need to get it together before we lose our chance
to change our government and society after we change ourselves
and correct our health
upon gaining knowledge of self
which is more important than material wealth
harness your Chi
open your third
then you will see you are no freer than a bird
in a cage that sings a song by Maya
check the words
if you don't know why the caged bird
sings
you can learn a thing
or two by watching nature
and studying ecology
to find out about the Earth
that cradles us from birth
to death
study the sociology
that stays hidden like the connections in ecology
we should know what connects us to nature
and every living and inanimate entity

that we pretend not to see
while driving in the city
such a pity
we can't see
the splendor of nature
or the truth behind the hype
given to US by those who type
or re-write and edit the news
that keeps us used
and abused
because we don't read behind the ~~deleted~~ scenes
to understand and know we haven't seen
a damn thing
that's legit
but we think we the shit
because we are too ignorant to view the facts
tagged to our backs
and soon to be on our mind
because we stay blind
to the truth and reality
we can't see the crime happening in "The City"
that affects US and the world
but we don't understand or know the science
so we overlook it like a damaged pearl
soon we will have to change
for the end is in range

## Senselessness

In a senseless country, everything makes sense and nothing makes sense.

*Why?*

The why would take as long to explain as the process that has brought senselessness to this country, as we are witnessing the last phases of the "New World Order."

*But I thought it was only a fairy tale from science-fiction books and movies?! Does it really exist?*

I am not telling you to think anything...I want you to think for yourself, something that few in this country do, as we are bombarded with what to think and how to feel through our parents, the 4-wall classroom education, the *corporament*'s media, and the government's mind control products and processes. If you don't believe me—I hope most of you don't—then do independent and thorough research to prove me right or wrong.

In this country, you tend to **see more robots than "freethinkers" as the robot-mentality is not limited to the**

**government and ~~defense~~ offense sectors**.

There are laws that prohibit the killing of humans, yet there are policies and initiatives (covert and overt) that allow and encourage the murder of humans. We are told that we fight wars to protect our "freedom," however, our freedom comes from the *Declaration of Independence* and *United States Constitution*! Not only that, the wars are fought by a department that has never been about defense, not even after it's name change in 1949.

We say that we want peace on Earth, but our "peace" missions are just a continuum of violence and destruction against people of color that live in countries with natural resources that our *corporament* desires. Nor can we forget our foreign policy that "saves" and "liberates" people by bombing and destroying their country.

It's past time for US to stop the senselessness that is prevalent in our country!

### Untitled — 03-06-02

My lyrics burn the pages of my notes
like the government made of people
that has continually burned
the citizens of this country
since its inception.
We need to stop
the exploitation, rather pimpin',
the continued slavery of our minds
through fluoride,
technology,
"schooling,"
the media,
society and the status quo
that keeps US ignorant.
For those 15...
percent, who are not sheep,
now is the time to spread the knowledge,
help others to break free,
to free themselves from the chains
they can't see,
and don't want to remove
for fear of no longer being "sane" or "normal."
But who decides, what's normal?
Why do they decide what's normal?
How do you know that the 15% are normal,
and not you?
Where do your thoughts
and thus, reality come from?
What aspect of technology brings it to you?

Or do you really think for yourself?
Don't front wit' me,
come real.
Before you answer...
think,
or can you even think for yourself?
If you were asked to "think outside the box,"
could you?

Do you even know what it means?
Have you ever had an original, or
a creative thought?
Or has all your creativity
been dissolved from your mind, body, and spirit?

Do you have,
what it takes to break free?
If you do,
join the revolution!

**Excerpt from <u>Who, What, When, How, Why? & Others</u>**

**(03-01-01) by Obiora Embry**

Why is money treated like a "God?"
Why is money worth more than human lives?
When did money become an integral part of our everyday lives
     and why?
Is it true that money is the root of all evil?


How can you sit back and watch as money
takes over your life and causes you and your family
     more hardships than war?
Is money necessary in our society or any society?
Will the destruction of the human race and
Earth come from the pursuit of money?


Why does the "American dream" make us believe
money will bring us
happiness and success?
Why do we confuse having or making
a lot of money with being successful?
Why does a person that is found (or deemed)
guilty of "crimes" have to pay fines to
the courts and government?
Does this really guarantee that "crime" will cease
or not be repeated?
Why are the individuals and groups whose pursuit for money
takes them into "illegal" activities
considered evil, are jailed, sent to prison,
     and/or put to death, when they were pursuing the
     "American dream?"

Does money bring a greater sense of happiness?
If not, then why are so many people's goals to make money?

How much does it cost to make clothes, toys, and shoes?
Why are some clothes, toys, and shoes so expensive,
even when made of
the same material and by the same manufacturer?
Why do we continue to support and
buy over-priced clothes, shoes, and toys?

Does the tag or name on your shirt
guarantee you a better quality than those
without the name tags and sold for less?
Does a product that is being sold for more money
than a similar product mean that the more expensive product
is of higher quality?
Why do tennis shoes cost so much, when most (if not all) cost
       less than $10 to manufacture?

Why does money cause so many problems?

# 2

## The Problem...continued

### Untitled — 07-19-00

Yo, the facility
be killing me
softly
like undetected AIDS,
creeping into your mind and body
causing your body to self-destruct
from the inside out.
No hope for help or cures,
price too expensive for the likes of us
to tango with.
Mad deep like bomb threats
or finding your government corrupt
from the top to the bottom.

Mega lies
told to cover up the untold truth
needed to be heard by the people of this country
and the world over.
Can I live?
Not if young, Black or Latino, poor, and male,
the government feels we are expendable,

setting us up to take the fall in the drug game,
knowing that's how some of us survive
and cope from day to day...
punishing us for crimes they created.
Drugs, guns, and loot being confiscated
and resold back into our communities.
It's a never-ending cycle and a battle
that's far deeper than good vs. evil.
Not every person you see as a friend is really
a friend,
not every person you see as your enemy is
an enemy.
The times changing
and the tides getting stronger.
Wish there was time for relaxation,
but the struggle continues.
Stay motivated and disciplined throughout life,
this will help you to cope with the tribulations of life.
No longer is it Black and white,
no real justice in a democracy,
especially not the racist and bias democracy
in which we live.
Democracy is not freedom,
more like oppression
and exploitation by the rich and wealthy.
A new economy is what's needed,
don't let US fool you into becoming a republic or democracy,
you will only regret it.
When you become a democracy,
it makes it easier for the U.S. to control and exploit you.

No need to let exploitation continue in this day and age,
need to stop corporations from running
sweat shops here and abroad
and from destroying the water and environment.
We need to survive as one race: the human race.
Survival by any means necessary,
sometimes life can get kind of hairy
and throw you curve balls
and bicycle-kicked balls,
shit hard to catch and handle.
I know that from the experiences I have had in my life.
But don't let that keep you from setting goals
and striving to achieve your dreams and goals.
Once you lose your ambition,
you lose your self
as you don't care whether you live or die,
for you have no reason to live.
It's deeper than kids killing kids
and babies having babies,
it doesn't take a psychology degree to figure that out.

A country bent on materialism and wealth,
telling its children that to become successful
you have to get a higher education,
and if you don't, you will never amount to anything.
Well for those of us who have tried
to get a higher education,
we need to tell the government how hard
it is when the tuition rises every year
and the amount that the federal and state
        governments spend on education decreases.

That's a linear relationship,
one that has a habit of cheating the youth and not so well off,
who get punished and outcasted trying to pay for school,
whether the people deem it moral, immoral, or illegal.
They are just trying to do what the slogan says:
          *stay in school.*
For those who don't get a higher education,
yet become successful,
I applaud you.
You figured out from the jump,
the education system is a brainwash,
from the beginning to end,
suffocating our individuality, creativity, and sometimes ambition.
With teachers and principals telling us
we will never amount to anything
or we can't do what our mind and heart want to.
It's got the youth going
coo-coo for cocoa
but not puffs
more like cocaine, heroine, acid, pills, and alcohol.
You heard of it,
they can name it and describe their effects.

On to bigger and better things,
like the corruption in our nation's capitol
and the evil that lurks behind
the walls of 'Corporate America.'
If only those walls could talk?!
Sadly I am sure most would be surprised by
what they have to say,

but even cynics would have to believe
because walls don't lie,
no matter how much you pay them.

Death threats,
they don't concern me,
they only bore me
tired of playing trivial pursuit with
wannabe thugs and killas,
playing hard to the next man
when they got a gun in hand.
Without the gun
the tough guy in you vanishes
like crack fiends being chased.
When will you learn that
guns were made to kill?
They weren't invented to save lives,
only to kill like other weapons of destruction.
If guns weren't made to kill,
then why are they illegal to conceal
in most states and all federal buildings?

I know what I am saying is drastic
but it's time for the knowledge to be spread
throughout the seven seas and the world.
Knowledge is power,
which can never be controlled or taken away,
and can be used as your defense when used properly.
Don't let a lack of information keep
you from making informed decisions.

Do your research,
check different sources
and be prepared to take a stand
when you see anything that's not right.
Don't be afraid to speak up or have your voice heard,
you will be amazed at how many people listen
and may even reach out a helping hand
to help you fight for the cause.
So long folks,
Adios, *[Spanish]*
alavidha (namaste), *[Hindi]*
Sayounara, *[Japanese]*
Au revoir, *[French]*
ma'assalama and As sala'amu alaikum, *[Arabic]*
do' da da go' hv i, *[Cherokee]*
haya, *[Swahili]*
Ka omesia or Ka odi. *[Ibo/Igbo]*

We are all ONE
under the Sun.
Don't let hate, prejudice, and ignorance become
the Achilles heel that destroys our world.

**Untitled — 2-12-02**

Stop the presses,
my life is already full of stresses,
no need to add to the distress
from the media spewing out propaganda
designed to fuel anger
in the hearts and minds of those without a clue
of what their country has done in their names
or what their country plans to do.
Who is to blame?

We need to stop the game
and continuum of violence
which threatens our world.
If we can't live in peace on this world,
then we have to change.
We can no longer stay the same;
we will need to change our thoughts
which have only brought
us millenniums of pain, suffering, and death.
We act wet
behind the ears
and keep each other in a perpetual state of fear
to further exploit Mother Earth,
the entity that gave us birth,
I think that it's a curse
that we act so vile
and then smile
in other people's face
while scheming to take his/her place

                    to be continued...

### Changes in the City

travelin' within such prosperity
amazed to see unlimited amounts of poverty
within the limits of the city
see lots of abandoned and neglected property
everywhere I go
don't you know
also seen burnt houses and buildings still standing
people demanding
change and improvement from their government
but the common lack empowerment
within the government of the city
even though they casted "votes" for the few that now run the
   city,
where is the sense in that?
how can we take away our responsibility to take care of our
   community?
gave it to those who run the city
but don't know the full extent of the problems where the people
   live at

Chorus:

*It's the city, such a pity*
*let's change, for the time is in range*
*to do our part before we no longer have a part*
*to play in our everyday choices and decisions,*
*who now makes the decision?*

several liquor stores and bars on each block
no wonder some people ain't in shock
as they drive through or around
must be too accustomed to hearing the sound
of multiple shot glasses hitting the table
leaving the impaired unable
to see the devastation and despair
but many do care,
they come from the city, across the "nation," and worldwide
to spark brain cells and plan city-wide
projects, demonstrations, protests, murals, and events
to educate and spark interest from others
to join the struggle, attend the next event
and bring others
to an awakening like Chopin or the Buddha
requires an open-mind, maybe even follow some dogmas of the
    religion named after the Buddha

Chorus:

*It's the city, such a pity*
*let's change, for the time is in range*
*to do our part before we no longer have a part*
*to play in our everyday choices and decisions,*
*who now makes the decision?*

the birthplace of the Ford Model T car
but you don't have to travel far
to damage your car
on the fucked up roads
that have more bumps than toads

even if you don't travel by car
you will be affected by the city plannin'
who did the plannin',
and why have the intersections and streets
been designed in the manner that exists on the streets?
some lights on the same line dance to different beats
making me wonder how many pedestrians and passengers die on
    the streets
some side streets
are no better than the more heavily ridden streets
hoping to see futuristic cars
running with no mechanical parts, therefore no petroleum
    needed for the car
innovation and imagination must have died with the Industrial
    Age
turn a page
into the future, what do you see?
You will see the bullshit you are accustomed to see-
ing every day, unless you decide like Sitting Bull
that "enough is enough" and the bull
must stop and be put to rest
the future now rests
on the shoulders of the living and unborn
to make a sustainable place to live for the next 7 generations of
        those unborn
do you really want your children,
grandchildren, great-grand children,
and so on and so forth
to survive 9 months in the womb and then be given birth
here, with the way it is now?
how can we love our children, but not want to begin making
        things better for them now?

Chorus:

*It's the city, such a pity*
*let's change, for the time is in range*
*to do our part before we no longer have a part*
*to play in our everyday choices and decisions,*
*who now makes the decision?*

Detroit has been many things to many people
"Detroit Red" aka Malcolm X, Harriet Tubman, Beulah Work, and
    Jimmy Boggs, to name just a few people
it was where I saw "The Weather Underground"
and the monument to the "Underground"
it is a city with lots of history
and now is the perfect time to begin the first chapter on the next
    300 years of history
start this chapter within your community
help to clean it up, repair the streets, etc., but most importantly
    bring back a sense of community
it's up to you to decide what role
you want to play in revitalizing the soul
of the city of Detroit,
yes, Motor City, Detroit

Chorus:

*It's the city, such a pity*
*let's change, for the time is in range*
*to do our part before we no longer have a part*
*to play in our everyday choices and decisions,*
*who now makes the decision?*

### Untitled — 1-20-03

Tired again,
bullshit still the same
just from different places and faces.
I don't think I can stand it any longer,
no I am not going anywhere.
I will not run and hide,
nor will I hold back and cry,
nor will I kill myself and die.

I plan to live a long life,
happiness comes from within,
it's found when I take away all of the turmoil
and pain
that radiates from my heart and soul.
Pain of losing, pain of staying alone,
or is it pain from being lonely?
Pain of a new day
in this world.

I can no longer sit back and watch,
nor can I act without thinking,
but I must act before it's too late.
But too late,
for what?
To create a new world
or a sustainable world?
How will the world react?
Do we really want peace and happiness,
or are they empty rhetoric and slogans?

When another child dies 3 seconds from now,
will those in the "richest" country care?
Or because they haven't been told to care, will they care?

Tired,
just plain tired,
got to get back my "Mojo" in time
to help renew and invigorate
this world of prejudice and hate.
I can't wait to rid the world
of animosity and jealousy from material wealth.

In the end,
who cares who wins or loses their soul
for the right to control and dominate a world
full of robots and non-thinkers?

# 3

## Interlude

**Untitled — 04-07-03**

What does it take for US
to wake up and discuss
the situation we find ourselves
in, should we blame ourselves
for being so gullible
and ignorant of the truth hidden behind the syllables,
told to keep US quiet and in order
so the ruling class can institute the new world order?

# 4

# Questions on Peace

### Untitled — 02-21-03

War and peace 'guised by the few
we don't know that our peace organizations
are comprised of members from the most destructive
and warmongering nations,
but because they use buzz words like *peace*
or have *peace* in their name,
we assume they care about supporting
and/or keeping the **peace**.
But what is peace?
How can we voice our desire for peace,
if we don't know what it is?
Is peace kept or created when a few nations,
sovereign states, territories, nation-states, and
captive lands have weapons
and the rest don't?
Tell me, how does this promote peace?

Can the United Nations promote and bring
about peace through weapons inspections when only
select countries are inspected?
If the purpose of the inspections is to

disarm countries for the promotion of peace,
then why aren't ALL countries with
known or suspected weapon production facilities,
research and development, storage, testing, and dealers
inspected by the U.N.?
Doesn't that make more sense than to
allow a few countries with known
aggression and hostilities toward other countries, religions,
"races" or ethnic groups decide who should
and shouldn't be inspected?

Is peace a process or an ideal?
Or is it both?
Can peace be achieved through the
processes/methods currently being used?
Or do the processes/methods cause more
struggle and conflict?
Can peace occur when there is conflict
in our hearts and/or when we individually
do not even have a peace of mind?

What are you doing to promote peace?
Have you resolved any and ALL past
conflicts with yourself and others?
Have you begun to place more value
on living creatures than on material goods
and possessions?
Have you started to love yourself,
if you don't already?
Have you walked a mile in someone else's shoes?
Have you tried to gain a better understanding

of cultures, people, and religions different from yours?
Or do you still harbor hate and contempt
for anything different from what you are
used to seeing or knowing?
If the latter is true,
then you have work to do
before seeking peace.

So let me ask again, can the United Nations
bring about peace?
Can an organization founded and based on
inclusion and exclusion bring about a
result based on compassion, respect, and understanding?
How can this organization bring about peace
when the majority of people in the country that
houses its headquarters do not have
respect, an understanding, or compassion for themselves
let alone people from other countries?
Is peace ever-lasting?
If so, then why have the "peace missions"
failed at creating a continuous peace?
What happens on these missions that keep
peace from occurring or lasting?
Does the current approach used for peace
need to be rethought?
What were the original and present thoughts
used by nations and *politrickcians*
to bring about peace?
Why haven't their past methods worked?
Were they designed to work or
were they intentionally made to fail?

Who benefits if they never work?
Do the warring factions, nations, tribes, families,
people, cities, towns, or territories benefit?
Or are the agencies, departments, organizations,
and people sent to help resolve the conflict benefitting?
Does anyone benefit emotionally
and spiritually from the present process?
Or all the benefits financial and social—depending
on who you know and who represents you,
if you are even represented in the peace process?

Can peace happen without US changing?
Or can we stay the same and still
bring about peace?
If the world seeks peace, then why
is there on-going research for more
destructive and technologically advanced weapons?
Shouldn't we seek peace by banning and stopping the
engineering design, research and development,
testing, and production of ALL new weapons and then
find ways to safely and effectively eradicate
all existing weapons and prototypes?

Why does the United States not have
a Department of Peace?
What was the original name of the Department of ~~Offense~~
        Defense?
Why was the name changed?
What did the past name suggest
about the foreign policy of the United States?
Is our foreign policy still based on *War*

or has it changed?
Has the U.S. as a nation changed
in a way that promotes compassion,
understanding, and peace?
Or does it promote fear, terrorism, anger, and imperialism?
When will the people of the United States
realize that they need to change their mindset,
consciousness, and ways?

When the TRUTH is revealed, can peace take over
after current hostilities are buried?
Or will the TRUTH bring about non-productive changes?
Regardless of what happens, the TRUTH has
to be awakened and the people of the world
have to be freed from the weight
that all of the lies have put on the world.

The TRUTH needs to "ring out from every mountaintop"
and be heard by ALL
so that real PEACE can begin
because right now peace is far from becoming reality
since we don't love ourselves,
love others,
and do not have compassion and respect for others,
nor do we try to understand other people,
which are the basic tenets that need
to be completed before PEACE can
stop being a dream and become a reality.

# 5

## War and Peace

**War, what's it good for?**

*War, what's it good for?*

Absolutely nothing.

I am dismayed at the elected officials of this country that feel more bloodshed needs to occur.  Haven't we already killed enough people?  There is no need to increase the pain and suffering of any nation nor the human race.

The cycle of violence that has been occurring for the past 200+ years of this country's existence, whether it be violence through war, battles and skirmishes, attacks, bombings, shootings, mass murders, genocide, weapons testing, the death penalty, synthetic drug research, or chemical/germ warfare needs to stop.

What message does this send to our children: when you have a problem with someone, instead of trying to work out the issue kill him/her? How would you feel if your child attempted to kill you or another relative because s/he could not resolve the issue without resorting to violence?

The above thoughts are some things that we need to discuss and think about before more unneeded bloodshed occurs.

## Death Penalty and War

"The President is merely the most important among a large number of public servants.  He should be supported or opposed exactly to the degree which is warranted by his good conduct or bad conduct, his efficiency or inefficiency in rendering loyal, able, and disinterested service to the Nation as a whole.  Therefore it is absolutely necessary that there should be full liberty to tell the truth about his acts, and this means that it is exactly necessary to blame him when he does wrong as to praise him when he does right.  Any other attitude in an American citizen is both base and servile.  To announce that there must be no criticism of the President, or that we are to stand by the President, right or wrong, is not only unpatriotic and servile, but is morally treasonable to the American public.  Nothing but the truth should be spoken about him or any one else.  But it is even more important to tell the truth, pleasant or unpleasant, about him than about any one else."

– Theodore Roosevelt

Okay let me get this straight.  We have laws in this country that prohibit the killing of another human being—with a penal policy that violates the law and allows the killing of those who "commit" certain crimes—so how can we justify the killing and assassination of people who live in another country, let alone this country?  Isn't it hypocritical for US to say that killing is illegal, yet it's justified when we are at "war?" How can we call ourselves "humans" when we cannot find other solutions to our problems besides murder?

I remember hearing arguments against the death penalty in which the opponents linked the death penalty (and murder) to acts of barbarism, and it was said to not exist within a "civilized" society.  But I wonder if people here even know the definition of the word "human," let alone "civilized."

This "infinite" war spoken about by our non-elected White House resident and his team of criminals has been planned for years and is different than the words typed by the complicit media.  This group needs to cover up their illegal past/present relationship with Saddam

Hussein and his regime. In addition, they plan to further manipulate the crude oil market, among other things but I have not uncovered the other reasons for this war yet.

Nonetheless, this war is illegal and immoral. The killing of civilians (children, women, and men), soldiers, and livestock cannot be justified in any context, especially not in the manner presented by this administration nor anyone else that supports this overt action of aggression and hostility—this lack of justification has been shown throughout history. The aggression will only lead to increased fear, anger, and resentment in "Iraq" and other countries.

## Death Penalty and Student Protest

There was a student protest in Tennessee; there was one casualty, a police officer. One suspect was arrested, a poor college student. He could not afford a lawyer, so he was appointed one by the court. He was found guilty of murder and *sentenced to death*. Through the public outrage incited by the media and rumors after the shooting, the town requested an immediate execution, which was granted.

It's now 15 years later...the student was executed by popular or public demand. Nonetheless, the case was reopened and evidence was brought forth that proved his innocence. In fact, friendly-fire was determined to be the true cause of the fatality.

The blood of an innocent person is on EVERYONE'S hand, everyone that chanted "execute him" and condemned the student until he was put to death. Yes, an innocent person was killed; justice was thought to have prevailed, but justice for whom and for what? The cop that pulled the trigger never had to appear in court; he never received punishment for his fatal mistake.

\*\*\*

This is a fictional story.  However, there have been over 70 criminal cases during the last 100 years that have resulted in an innocent person being sentenced to death row/and or executed.

When will public outrage lead to the abolition of the death penalty?  When will we stop allowing our government to kill in our names, leave the blood on our hands, and then call it "justice?"

It's time for US to think outside of the box. Let's do what's right, not just for this country, but for humanity to survive.

## 21st Century Holocaust

We are now witnessing the Holocaust of the 21st Century.  The scapegoat and the players have changed, but the rhetoric and method of extermination are practically unchanged.  The United States has now begun to use methods, tactics, and justifications that were borrowed from our past covert relationship with Adolf Hitler and his regime.  The new scapegoats are people that resemble or look like they are "Arabic" and/or Muslim, even though 60% of Arabs practice Christianity.  Nonetheless, we have and are allowing a tragedy that "black-listed" Germany to happen again.

The Nazis had concentration camps; we have the same, but we have been calling them "internment" camps since World War II.  Yet, the function remains the same: remove humans from society and perform inhumane acts on them.  We have heard about them and have seen news reports of the torture, beatings, and killings.  And I am sure that "illegal" experimentation—our government has been doing it for hundreds of years on US and others—may also be happening to the humans in the concentration camps.

Ever since Britain and the United States discovered crude OIL in what we now call the "Middle East," they have worked together with other European nations to embezzle it from countries in the Ottoman Empire with oil reserves. However, since many of the leaders in those countries have no desire for Western imperialism to continue, the United States and Britain have orchestrated *coup d'états*, assassinations, and political propaganda to control and manipulate the crude oil market.

Many of the leaders and citizens have refused to be threatened, coerced, manipulated, and controlled by US, therefore their religion had to be demonized. Through the demonizing of Islam, we have also succeeded in demonizing the people who practice it. Even though Christians are known for having the most degrading, violent, and dehumanizing system of slavery (which still exists today) the world has ever known, the religion and its people are untainted. However, when individuals or groups that practice Islam commit acts that we deem hostile, the individual(s) are blamed and so is their religion, why is this?

In this new Holocaust, the hatred for the scapegoat remains the same as the scapegoats have been blamed for many of the current "atrocities" in the United States and abroad.  They have been identified as the culprits, even when no evidence exists and the suspects are unknown.  And unpatriotically we have not questioned our government or held our elected officials accountable for not using due process of law.

Like Toni Morrison said in 2001, "we may be witnessing the Nazification of our country."  Yet, from where I stand, this is not the beginning, but rather the climax as we have justified our hatred for Muslims and the religion of Islam to the extent that another Holocaust is happening.

## Twice in a Lifetime

It is hard to fathom the idea that anyone who was not born before or during the first 2 World Wars would live through two acts of genocide twice in his/her lifetime. However, this is happening again, and to add more insult to this tragedy, this second genocide is happening on the same continent and almost 9 years after the first massacre began.

The first genocide began on April 6, 1994, in Rwanda—in central Africa—during 100 days. In the United States, we allowed the massacre to continue as our government officials ignored studies by the CIA and warnings from high military officers in the Rwandan Army released between December 1993 and January 1994 about the potential for widespread violence and disaster. President Clinton opposed the United Nations intervention that could have ended the genocide. And in May 1994, he signed a foreign policy directive that kept US from ending the slaughter.

We turned a blind eye to the atrocity because the Clinton

administration and the media never called the killings a *genocide*. If it weren't for the movie <u>Hotel Rwanda</u>, the massacre may have ended without US knowing about the "fastest, most efficient killing spree" of the 20th Century. The movie reenacted some of the atrocities that occurred during those 100 days, in which 800,000+ humans were murdered. Their deaths could have and should have been prevented by the United States and the United Nations.

Three years into the most recent conflict within Darfur, Sudan, there have been more than 400,000 deaths and 1,000,000 or more murdered while trying to escape. On the ninth of September 2004, then Secretary of State, Colin Powell, finally declared that we were witnessing another *genocide*. However, like many tragic events that take place in *The Motherland*, the media coverage is limited, but hopefully this will change as the massacre has now been covered by Oprah Winfrey.

On Wednesday, the twenty-sixth of April 2006, Oprah interviewed George Clooney, a Kentucky native and actor, about his recent trip to Sudan. He talked about the despair, the rapes, the starvation, other atrocities, and the need for the United States, the United Nations, and all humans to help put an end to the *genocide*. Oprah has included on her Web site [http://www.oprah.com/oprahshow/Humanitarian-Crisis/8] more information on the trip that George Clooney and his father made to Darfur, Sudan.

It is reported that 400,000 more humans have been murdered! It is not too late to help put an end to the continued massacres during this "ethnic cleansing." There are national and international groups that are working hard to provide aid to the countless victims and put an end to this 3-year *genocide*.

For more information, check out:

http://en.wikipedia.org/wiki/Darfur_conflict
"Darfur conflict"

http://www.darfurgenocide.org/
"Darfur: A Genocide We Can Stop"

http://www.washingtonpost.com/wp-dyn/articles/A8364-2004Sep9.hhtml

"U.S. Calls Killings In Sudan Genocide" *[no longer available]*

http://www.cbsnews.com/stories/2004/10/08/60minutes/main648277.sshtml

"Witnessing Genocide In Sudan" *[no longer available]*

http://topics.nytimes.com/top/news/international/countriesandterritories/rwanda/index.html?offset=285&s=newest

"Critics Say U.S. Ignored C.I.A. Warnings of Genocide in Rwanda"

http://mediafilter.org/MFF/CAQ/CAQ52Rwanda.html

"U.S. Complicity by Silence: Genocide in Rwanda"

http://www.pbs.org/wgbh/pages/frontline/shows/evil/

"frontline: the triumph of evil"

http://www.gwu.edu/~nsarchiv/NSAEBB/NSAEBB53/press.html

"The U.S. and the Genocide in Rwanda 1994"

http://www.theatlantic.com/doc/200109/power-genocide

"Bystanders to Genocide"

http://notonourwatchproject.org/

"Not On Our Watch"

# 6

# The *Police* and Peace

## Excerpt from <u>Who, What, When, How, Why? & Others</u> (4-25-01)

### by Obiora Embry

Why is it deemed justifiable and appropriate for cops/police
    officers to kill other cops (friendly-fire) and citizens?
Why do cops kill?
Are they not taught to maim or slow down someone running
    or reaching for a weapon?
If not, why not?
Why do cops kill first and ask questions last?

Why are police officers being military trained?
What can we as citizens, taxpayers, and voters do to stop these
    killings and beatings of unarmed people?
Why do we let this continue?
How many more must die or get beat up before we realize
    something is wrong and needs to be changed?
Will you, a friend, or a family member have to be killed or beaten
    by a cop before we realize that things have to change?

Who's here to protect us from the cops when they decide to use
    excessive force, shoot multiple shells, and/or murder us?

Do the police have too much power?
If so, then why don't limit their power?
Are cops above the law or do they uphold the law?
What happens when that line is crossed and citizens and/or
     immigrants are murdered?
Is a police officer's life more important than ours,
     is that why it's acceptable for a cop to take our last breath,
     appear in court and then be acquitted for single or
     multiple homicides?

Do the police or soldiers deserve recognition or honors/awards
     for the number of people they kill or the number of times
     they shoot their guns?

Does violence create peace?
If not, how does the continued use of the death penalty
     and cops killing us create peace?
Why are these hypocrisies allowed to persist?
Why do the police carry and/or use assault rifles, automatic,
     and/or semi-automatic weapons?
Who are they fighting?
Are the police being trained to kill or to help and heal?
Can cops protect us by using violence against us?
Will we be able to stop the next murder by a police officer?
Are the police needed to create harmony and peace?
Are there any alternatives to the police?

What will happen to our communities if martial law begins?
Will we be ready?
Who will fight to stop this from happening?

## 5-O

The pigs,
the fuzz,
one-time,
po-po,
the beast
are names that we have used for police officers or cops.
But what they really should be called are protectors of
      aristocrats[2],
as that is how they started and what they are returning to.
Two questions must now be asked in the
wake of police shootings and beatings
that have happened all over this country:
      Who are the police here to protect?
      And are the same people they swear to protect,
      the same people they serve?
Without this knowledge,
it is hard to review a system
that you're on the outside looking in on.
I am not saying that all cops are bad,
but I am saying something needs to be done.
Who knows, the next casualty,
could be you, a friend of yours,
or maybe even me?
You never know,
with all of the racial profiling
and ignorance in today's world,
nobody's life is promised to survive each day,
and this is especially true if you are a person of color.

Just keeping it real,
but at the same time,
don't believe everything you hear,
check to see if there's truth in what gets
relayed to your ears.
Do your research and don't get caught up in the hype.

They tell us to trust the police
and to put our lives in the cop's hand
when trouble or danger appears.
But what happens,
when the trouble or danger appears
from a cop(s)?
Who can you call to protect you?
Will anyone believe you?
Most of the country is so blind with patriotism,
they can't see and don't want to believe
the wrongdoings that are going on
under their eyes and noses.

When cops become corrupt
or turn into vigilantes,
it's past time to question the policies and regulations
that give them their power, and so much power
that they begin to feel and act
like they are invincible.
This has been proven time after time,
as cops have been acquitted of criminal charges,
no matter how strong the evidence is/was against them.
Something is wrong,
it's past time we wake up and realize

something needs to be changed.
This B.S. needs to stop,
or has the problem been ignored by
a society that advocates violence,
but at the same time condemns it?
It's hypocritical,
if you think about it.
It's against the law to kill people,
but the death penalty makes it legal to kill people,
in which the majority of them have been Black.
It's almost like a modern-day Holocaust
in which our society
is cleansing itself of Black males.

Cops, the lesser of two evils,
but what's the other evil?
Society itself is bias,
making the justice system bias and blind
to the prejudice and discrimination
that happens within the confines of the system.

2. "COMMUNITY-ORIENTED POLICING: HISTORY."
http://what-when-how.com/police-science/community-oriented-policing-history/

## Untitled — 09-21-03

*Violence only begets violence*
*talk of murder on wax followed by silence*
*doesn't cause violence*
*and couldn't logically in a country with a history of violence*

now all you hear is silence
as those around you contemplate
to begin the debate
on music and violence

driving down the block
where Tony Sullivan was shot
by the cops
wondering if his death at the hands of cops
was or would be blamed on hip-hop
if not,
why not?
he was killed by violence
cops got off as another one of us has been silenced
why the madness
from the sadness
of another casualty of color
by the crew sporting the blue color?
close friends, associates, and others went buck wild
but in a different way from "girls gone wild"
we were hot with anger
felt we could no longer trust the stranger
sworn to protect and serve

they plucked our nerves
and sent fear multiplied by two
to others who went through
bull shit with cops
but they weren't shot
to death
couldn't hold out for one last breath
now what's the penalty for death
after you take away someone's last breath?

unless you a part of the crew
dressed in blue
not talkin' about the Crips
who kill if a nigga set-trip

*Violence only begets violence*
*talk of murder on wax followed by silence*
*doesn't cause violence*
*and couldn't logically in a country with a history of violence*

# 7

## Parents

### Gardening and Parents

This year it is imperative that we as parents and caregivers begin to change the relationship that our children and other youth have with Nature, and the relationships that they have with each other and us. One such method of bringing about a positive transformation is to re-connect them with Nature.

It has been reported that our children are suffering from "nature-deficiency." Our children can ameliorate this deficiency by spending less time indoors and more time outside interacting with other youth, breathing fresh—moving—air, playing, or interacting with Nature on a deeper, more personal level through starting or renewing an urban or rural garden.

Some of the benefits from gardening include: providing your family with fresh locally grown fruit, vegetables, and herbs; developing a greater awareness and appreciation for Nature; finding or renewing your sense of self and purpose; becoming more responsible, patient, loving, and nurturing; increasing your attention span; and applying subject material from school to real-life.

## Excerpt from <u>Who, What, When, How, Why? & Others</u>

## (4-5-01/4-16-01) by Obiora Embry

Why do we hurt and abuse children that we help to bring into
    this world?
Why do we let others hurt and bring harm to our children?
What can we do to keep our children from harm, besides keeping
    them locked inside our home?
Does sheltering children keep them "out of harm's way?"
If not, then why do parents continue doing it?

Why do we shower our children with material goods?
How do you punish a child by sending him/her to his/her room
    full of the latest "entertainment products" that the media
    and big companies influence our children and/or ourselves
    to purchase?

Why are so many of the youth unruly or show a lack of
    respect to their elders, especially their parents?
Where do we as fathers stand in all of this?
Where do parents, the community, and relatives
    stand in all of this?
Why do parenting magazines and books cater primarily to
    mothers?
Why don't they have articles and books that are written to
    include both parents, the mother and father?
Why are the courts and social workers biased against fathers?
Why is it hard to believe that fathers can raise their children solo
    or with the help of the mother?

Why do kids have kids when they do not have the physical,
emotional, mental, or financial ability to raise babies?
And why do their parents and/or guardians allow it to keep
happening?
Do these children not use contraceptives?
If they do, were they used properly?
Have their parents or guardians taken the time to discuss sex:
the good, the bad, and the truth with their children?
Why do children feel they have to have sex before they are
ready?
Why are less children waiting to have sex until after they get
married?
Where is the pressure coming from?
Why is it okay for guys to be promiscuous, but not females?
Why is it cool to have more than 1 sex partner, especially
with the recent epidemic of deadly STDs?
Why are children becoming sexually active at younger and
younger ages?
Why are so many males over 18 having sex with and/or fathering
children with females just entering middle school and/or
high school?
Do the parents of these girls know their daughters are dating
and/or sleeping with older guys?
If so, why is it allowed?
Is sex a substitution for love or is it an extension of love?


Have any parents sat down and watched any of the new cartoons
and other TV shows designed for children?
If so, why are they still on the air?
Why do so many of these TV shows display ethnic stereotypes
and myths?

## Untitled — 1/12/2004

Trapped in a time zone
tryin' to find time alone
truth buried like a bone
kids tryin' to hone
their bodies, developing early
minds not developing early
kids growing too fast
with the way they progressing
human race may not last
technology progressing
life at faster rates
humanity decreasing at faster rates
welcome to the future...dates on T.V.
we no longer have privacy
things no longer the way they used to be
parents can't see
the forest for the trees
so kids put in jeopardy
schools not helping to educate
standards seem to debilitate
hurting the students most disadvantaged
packing years of content into 1 year
not just those disadvantaged
leaving the system
that has dissed them
led them astray
telling them there is only 1 way
to gain knowledge, discipline problematic
causin' more movement than electrons with electricity that's static

teachers stressed out like jammed automatics
weaponry is fear, chaos in the classroom
who's to blame when problems are swept like a broom?
kids slippin' through the cracks is automatic
overcrowded classrooms with underpaid teachers
who often can't reach her
or him, me, or you,
what are da parents to do?
we got to get through
to officials in charge and run through
the problems our kids facin'
time is racin'
and running out
like scared kids with the lights out

### Excerpt from <u>Times Done Changed</u>

Who's to blame for the youth
killing each other
over chump change
and overpriced clothes and shoes?
Society and the media repeating
age-old stereotypes to the youth of today,
keeping ignorance, despair, misunderstanding, and hatred alive.
Are society and the media the only to blame
for the problems the youth face today?


Where do, we as parents fit
into all of the self-hatred and disrespect
shown by our children, grandchildren, cousins, nieces, nephews,
      and youth of the community?
Where were we when our children needed us the most?
Were we at work, out on a date, asleep, or just not around?
Why have we let the TV, television specials and shows, and our
      caregivers,
take on the responsibility of caring for and raising our children?
When did we stop caring or stop having the time to parent
and be there for our children?
Why do we have children,
when we can't give them what they need?


Our children are now living in a world bent on promoting
arrogance, ignorance, sex, greed, materialism, and lies
because it wants to market to the biggest spenders,
the youth.
This ain't no jive,

as our youth struggle to survive
and live to adulthood.
Bombarded by drugs, sex, violence, hatred,
        and ignorance from all over,
confused about life and the way things are and
the way things used to be,
they struggle to survive from day to day,
wishing at times they were dead or had never been born,
as the life they are living is no fairy tale or Disney cartoon.
Having to deal with real life situations on a daily basis,
angered when their teachers tell them
after they graduate from high school or college
that they will enter the real world,
even though many students live in the real world now.

Times done changed
and the world's a scary place to be.
But take it from me,
the seasons change
and with time our mindsets will change,
maybe to realize that something must be done.

# 8

## Finding Peace Through Knowledge

**Untitled — 10-9-00**

Knowledge is the key
many do not use
to unlock themselves from the abuse
they are witness to, either you or me
are the ones that can help
but we stand motionless and can't be seen like stealth
caring more about our own wealth
than the health
of another
why is it so hard to treat your fellow man like a brother?
respecting him for who he is
and treating your fellow woman like your sis
respecting her like you should respect your Mom

Stay calm
don't be alarmed
all will be well
as I am dropping the jewels
that cannot be fooled

**Connect the D.O.T.S.**

Web version with resources available @

http://utgift.freehostia.com/connect_dots.pl

We the people, the inhabitants of the United States and the Earth, have a responsibility to solve the problems that we helped to create when we allowed the visual and aural propaganda to influence our daily thoughts and decisions because we were blinded and disillusioned by greed, fear, ignorance, arrogance, and a lack of respect for the Earth (that we inherited from our ancestors and will pass on after we expire).

We owe it to the unborn and yet to be thought of, to rediscover what it means to be "human," responsible, to work together and solve problems, to distinguish fact from fiction, to recognize that not everyone in this country has the same "standard of living," and that all change must begin with ourselves.

We must demand that automobile manufacturers quit playing "brand new" when it comes to non-gasoline powered vehicles. Henry

Ford's first Model T ran on ethanol produced from *industrial hemp* and everything except for the steel frame was plant-based. The Model T was built using a combination of flax, wheat, industrial hemp, spruce pulp, and soy beans. Rudolph Diesel, the "inventor" of the diesel engine worked on the idea of a solar engine between 1880 and 1890. In 1900, he unveiled a diesel engine that ran on peanut oil at the World's Fair Exposition in Paris, France. The research, automobiles, and ideas of Ford, Diesel, and countless others should already be known to automobile manufacturers. However, for us to understand why this "technology" has been stifled for so long, we must first understand the continuum that began after Sir Percy Cox and others carved up the Ottoman Empire and created the "Middle East" after World War I.

The new boundaries created within the Ottoman Empire were designed to guarantee conflict and keep the region divided so oil concessions and royalties would be easier to negotiate. The instability created within the "Middle East" combined with a petroleum shortage fear in the 1920's, the *Red Line Agreement* of 1928, and corporations defining policy in Washington, D.C. helped to spiral a domino effect nationally and internationally that still exists today.  [*The Red Line Agreement* gave the Near East Development Corporation (consortium of 5 large United States petroleum companies) 23.75% of the Turkish Petroleum Company's shares in the new British mandate, Iraq, and joint development of other petroleum fields within the *Red Line.*]

This continuum has coexisted with and has been a primary cause of the following:
· tax on marihuana—Marihuana Tax Act, which made it easier for industrial hemp and marihuana to be prohibited nationally,
· an increase in the usage of petrochemicals and synthetics in the fiber and food industries,
· resurgence of the Ku Klux Klan and increased racial tension in the United States towards Mexicans and Blacks through the national propaganda created to demonize marihuana,
· an increase in domestic policies dictated by corporations rather than US (i.e., water fluoridation and a national prohibition on industrial hemp and marihuana),
· petroleum fueled automobiles,

· plant-based products almost eliminated as competition in the "paper," paint, plastics, textile, and automotive industries,

· greater reliance on petroleum and its derivatives,

· less fuel efficient automobiles and collusion between petroleum and automobile companies,

· discrete government, banking, business, and private partnerships with countries that have natural resources (i.e., Panama, Iran, Iraq, Saudi Arabia, South Africa, Afghanistan, etc.),

· greater dependence on "state-sponsored terrorism" and war to control and gain access to the world's natural resources,

· increase in air, water, and land pollution by corporate "America",

· and the rise of the *corporament* (government + corporations) that we must dismantle, if *we the people* should continue to be significant.

Furthermore, we must demand that companies clean up their act. They must clean up the bodies of water they have polluted, which can be accomplished through the use of phytoremediation and/or bioremediation. Companies must reduce the inflated paychecks of upper management. In addition they need to redesign their processes, products, and infrastructure using the principles of Nature as a guide, and eliminate toxic by-products, emissions, pieces, and parts from their manufactured goods. And lastly, all businesses must take their money out of the politicians' pockets at the town/city/county, state, and federal levels.

We the people must demand that the acts and laws that have been passed due to flimsy and circumstantial evidence, fear, and ignorance like the Marihuana Tax Act, Controlled Substances ACT, Patriot ACT, and RAVE ACT be repealed.

We must also change the view that we have of Mother Earth, our neighbors, the businesses that we patronize, our employers, our lifestyles, and our mindsets. We must overcome our ignorance, fear, greed, and lack of understanding of the world in which we live, and change the source(s) that we use to obtain our news. Ultimately, we must remove the control that the *corporament* has on our daily lives.

### Untitled — 02 April 2003

I speak on a level,
few can understand or handle,
but I got more knowledge about you
than you have about yourself.
Isn't it sad that you don't know
a damn thing about yourself?
Where did we go wrong,
individually,
and as a society
so that we don't know a damn thing
about ourselves,
let alone people from different backgrounds?
How can we change the world for the better,
when we don't have peace in our hearts and minds?
Where can we find
peace,
if we don't even know internally what peace is?
Are we so disillusioned that we
can't think straight or logically?

What is the reason for our ignorance
of ourselves?
Where did we go wrong?
What can we do to change
our current situation?
Can we find happiness and pleasure externally, if we don't have
        them internally?
Or are we so removed from "real" happiness and pleasure
that we can't distinguish "fact" from "fiction?"

Should we start looking internally
for peace
or should we seek it elsewhere
and then bring it inside?

We need to open our eyes to the
inconsistencies of the stories presented
to our senses,
and use our third eye to distinguish
fact from fiction.
Then we need to seek peace within ourselves.

## Untitled — 10-15-02

Let's set the record straight
there can still be a debate
but I already know my fate
and destiny, I am destined to be martyred
however, right now I really don't care
I am still going to give it to you while saying fuck the world of
        material wealth
more devastating than the radiation effects of stealth
bombing the globe and the people don't even know
it's a shame
but we have no one to blame
but ourselves
we need to disarm our weapons of mass destruction
and quit seeking the destruction
of other cultures
that are misunderstood by the populace
of the "U.S. culture"
Instead we need to arm the populace
with knowledge of self
and the laws of our country, better yet the laws of Nature by
        which we should live
we can give
as much as we please, but until we take the knowledge that
        others give
we are left without a real reason to live

# 9

## Spiritual Search

### Self-knowledge

There are three films that should be included in the next Literature of the Spiritual Search class.  They are <u>Circle of Iron</u> (aka <u>The Silent Flute</u>), <u>The Matrix</u>, and <u>Kung Fu: The Movie</u>.  In each movie the main character goes on a spiritual search through different means.  The spiritual searches and the underlying philosophical messages can spark intellectual classroom discussions.  In addition, the movies can enlighten the class about different groups and viewpoints that are rarely encountered in this country.

The <u>Circle of Iron</u> was co-written by the legendary Bruce Lee.  It is different from the other movies that he wrote and/or starred in because <u>The Silent Flute</u> has only a small number of fighting scenes.  Instead the movie deals primarily with the main character Cord and his philosophical revelations. Cord enters a fighting contest to become the Seeker of Zetan, "the Keeper of The Book" that holds the secrets of the Universe and information to become Enlightened. Cord is disqualified because he did not follow the rules, however, he continues on his quest to find Zetan and "The Book." During his search, Cord faces 3 moral and ethical obstacles that were put in his way to test and challenge him. Each obstacle that Cord overcame changed the way he viewed himself and the world around him. When he finally reaches Zetan and views "The Book" (of Enlightenment) Cord ends his spiritual search.

Cord's spiritual search is similar to the one that Neo, the main character, in The Matrix experiences. Neo spends his nights trying to find the secret of the *Matrix* and through another hacker, Trinity, he meets Morpheus, who becomes his mentor and guide. At the initial meeting, Morpheus describes the *Matrix* as "the world that has been pulled over your eyes to blind you from the truth." In taking the red pill offered by Morpheus, Neo is able to continue his search for the truth. Morpheus tells Neo that he is *The One*, but Neo does not believe it. Morpheus is captured by the agents of the *Matrix*, so Neo and

Trinity return to the *Matrix* to save him. Morpheus and Trinity escape, so Neo faces his biggest battle with the agents by himself. It is during this fight that Neo realizes the truth about his fate and also the *Matrix* thus ending his spiritual awakening.

Kung Fu: The Movie is different from the other two movies because the main character, Kwai Chang Caine (or Caine) is a Shaolin priest, who is already spiritually enlightened. In the movie, set in 1885, Caine is with his teacher, Master Po when he is shot and killed by an escort of the Royal House. Caine is enraged by this action and kills the *escort*, who is the Royal Nephew. Caine escapes to the "Old West." There Caine is confronted by an assassin, Chung Wang and The Manchu, who is the father of the Royal Nephew. Before Caine's duel with his son, the assassin, Caine receives another lesson from Master Po. At the end of the movie, Caine goes from being a *pupil* to the *teacher* after he gives his son, Chung Wang his first lesson.

The Matrix, Kung Fu: The Movie, and Circle of Iron are important for learning about viewpoints and a group not normally discussed in this country. This group consists of those that study and use martial arts in its purest form. And more importantly, they know that martial arts is a way of life that helps to enlighten and connect their minds, bodies, and spirits. In each movie, martial arts plays a role within the life of the main character. The main characters are disciplined, patient, humble, and wise, which are characteristics that are developed over time by martial artists. In addition, a lot of the philosophy and spirituality in martial arts comes from Buddhism.

Since there is a connection between Buddhism and martial arts, a martial artist is often a spiritual person. I cannot think of any sport or activity with roots in the West that incorporates the mind, body, and spirit. For people in the West to further understand this connection, horizons need to be expanded and more should learn about the philosophical and spirituality of martial arts.

There is an underlying Buddhist philosophy that appears in each film. It is "all that we seek is within." This concept of a spiritual search is different from the ones that we have discussed in class because most of the works, if not all, the search for the spiritual occurred externally. A student posed a question in class about the possibility of a person going on a spiritual search without physically going anywhere. This is possible and even though the main characters go on a physical journey, the spiritual search begins and ends within themselves.

The characters of Cord, Neo, and Caine understand that being happy does not come externally but rather from within. They also recognize the connection between spirituality and Nature. Possibly after seeing Kung Fu: The Movie and Circle of Iron others will see the connection between spirituality and Nature. This idea of being connected can foster discussions on whether one can be spiritual or become spiritually awakened without reconnecting or connecting with Nature.

The other difference from works discussed this semester is that spiritual searches have nothing to do with religion. In many of the books that we read, the main character goes on a search via a religion. In the movies, none of the main characters use religion as a basis for their respective searches. And these movies allow one to understand that a spiritual search is a journey that begins and ends with oneself, therefore it is unique to each person.

Religion and technology have been used to coerce, control, and enslave others throughout history. In <u>The Matrix</u> humans are enslaved by the hands or rather the mind of *machines* through a computer simulation (the *Matrix*). The humans that have not unplugged from the mental imprisonment created by the *Matrix* believe that what they see, touch, smell, taste, and hear is real but in reality it is only an illusion, a computer simulation that only exists within their minds. This illusion was crafted to keep them mentally enslaved so that the machines could utilize their collective body heat and bioeletrical energy.

This is similar to our world. Many still foolishly believe that everything they see, touch, hear, taste, and smell is real, even when there is doubt. Only when we begin to understand that our doubt is there for a reason will we become open to seeking the truth. After the search for the truth begins, one will slowly but surely come to the realization that what they once perceived to be real is not but rather a Jedi mind trick or an optical illusion of the mind.

The technology that exists today is artificial and has been designed and developed to create a virtual world or reality. If humans continue to develop machines to do our jobs then what will happen to us after these machines develop a mind of their own with the help of Artificial Intelligence (AI)? If this happens, there is a possibility that the Matrix—a reality beyond reality that controls every aspect of one's life—could take over our lives and become the source of what we perceive to be real. If this were to happen, it would be almost impossible to distinguish fact from fiction.

The problems that stem from our artificial technology are important to understand when talking about a spiritual search because it has the capacity to cause humans to become further disconnected from Nature, and over time there is the possibility that more people will seek a different reality. However, it will be harder to find as one will have to break through the artificial layers stored within the mind in an effort to come face-to-face with reality. After someone makes technology a part of their everyday life, s/he is likely to become less connected with Nature, which means that it will be almost impossible for a spiritual search to happen.

Works Cited

Circle of Iron.  Dir. Richard Moore (III).  Perf. David Carradine, Christopher Lee, and Jeff Cooper.  1997.  Videocassette.  Mia Video Entertainment Ltd, 1978.

Kung Fu: The Movie.  Dir. Jerry Thorpe.  Perf. David Carradine, Barry Sullivan, and Albert Salmi.  1998.  Videocassette.  Warner Studios, 1972.

The Matrix.  Dir. Andy Wachowski and Larry Wachowski.  Perf. Keanu Reeves and Laurence Fishburne.  2000.  Videocassette.  Warner Studios, 1999.

## Spiritual Search

We have gotten our priorities wrong. Over the years we have begun to value ourselves and each other less because our primary focus has been making money or becoming *successful*. The shit has hit the fan because parishioners now also have a similar focus. These turbulent times have caused the search for the spiritual to become even more prevalent. However, the spiritual search that I am referring to does not include one's search for a religion to believe in and/or practice.

Religion and spirituality are not synonyms. Religion—especially the practising of it—is external; it is not a part of one's being. The Judeo-Christian religion, which most people in this country practice was one of the first religions that removed (the Universal) *God* from the Earth, gave it a human form, and a sex. By putting *God* in heaven and placing an emphasis on eternal life in heaven, Earth has been looked at as a stepping stone. This attitude has allowed followers of Christianity to desecrate to the Earth because they do not regard it nor its inhabitants as sacred. This belief contradicts older religions and spiritual beliefs that understand that *Mother Earth* and all of her inhabitants are sacred and have their own spirit/energy.

It is possible for a person to be spiritual and religious at the same time. However, it is more common for someone to only be one or the other. I have observed that many religious people rarely practice the beliefs contained within their religious doctrines 24/7. They also may make judgement calls about how other people choose to live their lives, even though they do not always practice what they preach! In addition, too many only worship their *God* or behave morally and ethically on their Sabbath—assuming that it even happens then!

However, when one decides to become spiritual, the search that s/he goes on creates an awakening that embodies the whole person. Once one reaches this state, s/he does not act divine from time to time, rather the person consistently acts morally and ethically, as it becomes an intricate part of that person. There is no longer a division between the mind, body, and spirit. It is recognized and understood that the three are one.

In order for this to happen, a person needs to develop a new train of thought. One should begin to realize that s/he is connected to everything that can and cannot be seen within the Universe. This thinking is not limited to Eastern thought, religions, and beliefs. There have been many non-Eastern people that have reached the same conclusion, and this is especially true with indigenous people. Two of the most famous people from the West that reached the same conclusion are Albert Einstein and Leonardo da Vinci.

In a sense, they may have gone on a spiritual search. You may be wondering, how? There is not a concrete definition of a spiritual search. Each person has a *flute* that only s/he can hear that acts a guide while searching for the spiritual, therefore, the path taken is different for everyone. However, when one's journey ends s/he will think, act, and view the world differently.

Contrary to popular belief and to those within our class, the spiritual search is not always done by those who are poor and/or unhappy with their life. Anyone can go on a spiritual search. During the search, a person will begin to look at everything with a completely different perspective, which includes the realization that we are all one! After developing a new perspective, s/he can become unhappy or dissatisfied with their life.

After this awakening, one realizes that we collectively cannot continue to sustain a society nor a world in which money is the primary focus, with the pursuit of money leading people to commit immoral, unethical, cruel, and/or deadly acts. We as humans cannot survive on material goods alone. There has to be a spiritual element within our lives. Once a person takes time to contemplate life and its meaning, s/he may feel dissatisfied and angry, thus one may seek a new way of life or thinking. This transformation can lead to a spiritual awareness and allow one to become more human.

There is a belief in our society that we become human through the process of birth, but there is a lot more to it. Being human takes a spiritual awakening and/or enlightenment and regarding other people, the Earth, and its inhabitants as sacred since we all come from a divine source through which we are all connected.

Many who follow the ways of the world, act immorally and unethically, and do not care about or respect anything are not acting like a human. For humanity to survive, we collectively and individually must develop a compassion for all living creatures. However, this compassion is only a small part of one's potential spiritual awakening.

Searching for the spiritual is different for everyone. As with most things in life, there is no standard because we are all unique. There could be six billion different ways of performing a spiritual search, it just depends on your frame of mind when you begin searching.

For instance, during the past year, I have been on a spiritual search. However, I was not conscious of this until recently. I began searching for the truth and started to question the current conditions and practices of societies, especially those of our hypocritical and unjust society. In addition, I began to re-evaluate my own life, my destiny, and my true purpose, this lifetime. Even though I can never forget my past nor who I used to be, I do know that I am not that person any more and my life experiences have helped me to become the person who I am today.

I have flipped the script and instead of trying to destroy the Earth and her creatures, I have come full circle. I have changed how I think and view the world. I have redefined many of the words that I once used. And in doing so, I had to recreate the vocabulary I use to express myself.

I have had to re-evaluate many things, especially the notion of being human and my personal belief system. I did not and do not want to be like the parishioners that follow a religion and its doctrine blindly. I want to live a life that makes sense and embraces compassion and truth, rather than deceive others and not be true to myself.

Buddha was once asked whether he was *God* or a man. He responded and said, "Neither. I am awake." This awakening is the climax of a spiritual search. At this junction, one has found the enlightenment and truth that was sought. One also realizes that there is no separation between body, mind, and spirit, and on a larger scale, the Earth and everything on it. This awakened individual has a greater sense of self and realizes that every action taken affects the equilibrium of the Earth.

If a person continues on the spiritual search after enlightenment is found, then there is the possibility s/he will reach Nirvana. When a person finds Nirvana there will be an internal peace which will exude throughout his or her body. This inner peace can and will be felt with every action and word that s/he expresses.

Life is a circle and after one realizes that s/he is a part of the Earth and vice versa, then one realizes that there is no separation between the two. And more importantly there will be an understanding that there is no me vs. the Earth or the Earth vs. her inhabitants because we are all inter-connected and intertwined like a spider web. Large and unbalanced movements or damage to a strand will affect the whole web. The appreciation, compassion, love, and understanding gained from a spiritual search can quell any battle that once raged inside because there is now an inner peace, thus ending the search for the spiritual.

# 10

## The Present, Future...and Change

**Change through...**

Think about the products you currently use to clean your house, automobile, or garage...these products usually have only one (1) suitable/usable function such as cleaning windows, floors, ovens, toilets, carpets, etc.  Think about how much money you could save and how much better your health would be if you had been informed about non-toxic and multi-tasking products that can perform all of those tasks and more.  But having this mind set and being an informed citizen can wreak havoc on businesses that promote toxic and/or hazardous one-time use or disposable products.

We have been told by the *corporament* (government + corporations) that by not supporting transnational businesses and corporations the economy would be weakened, workers would be laid off, and we would have to engage in another war stimulate the economy.  If this changed mindset were to become mainstream, then corporations would ~~bribe~~ lobby Congress to create laws that limit or prohibit the sale or usage of non-toxic, non-hazardous, and multi-tasking products.

The above action by corporations helps to explain one of the causations that led to the  prohibition of marihuana.  The industrial giants of the early 20th Century saw industrial hemp and its cousin, marihuana as a threat to the livelihood of their businesses, their lifestyles, and way of life.  These industrialists through the media companies they owned persuaded US that we could not live without their products, so we bought them and made them richer and us poorer.

What has/did this blind and uniformed consumerism do for US?

Through the alliance of the corporament, our $H_2O$ has been strategically contaminated with poisons like fluoride, chlorine, arsenic, lead, mercury, dioxin, etc.  Our land, air, and water has been and is still being poisoned. This widespread poisoning has led to an increase in the occurrence of cancer and other dis-eases. In addition, it has adversely altered our minds, sense of perception, our connection with each other and the way in which we view the world, which has kept too many of us from standing up to the companies that are destroying the natural balance of our planetary ecosystem.

## News Diary

Injustices to the max,
no time to relax
or unwind,
just got enough time to kick the facts.
If you don't believe,
watch for the signs,
the coming of a new day.
Revolution will take us there,
the 2nd one in this country's history,
but the one that will bring about the most changes
and have the biggest impact on all her people,
not just those with pale skin.
If you are tired of witnessing injustices to your own people
or another ethnic group,
Then it's time to:
"Get up,
stand up for your rights"
and "by any means necessary."

A future without you,
a future without me looks scary
like a child witnessing violence for the 1st time
or a baby learning how to walk.
Just listen to the news and you will have
reasons to be scared or angered.
Listen to what's going on in your neighborhood, city, state, country,
        and the world.
"Temperatures rising" like Mobb Deep.
Cops killing innocent citizens and immigrants

without probable cause.
Kids killing kids and school administrators.
Gas prices rising with no hope coming from the government to lower
    them.
Executions through the death penalty increasing every year.
Colleges and universities turning into businesses.
Increases in legal drugs and prescription drugs that are as
deadly and addictive as the drugs
America scrutinizes and keeps illegal.
America's youth are realizing the hypocrisies of their nation,
and males are realizing they are expendable and can be gotten rid of at
    anytime,
especially if you are Black.

America needs to realize drugs are not the problem,
they are the solution to the user's problem(s).
Until they realize this,
they will be fighting a losing battle,
as it's the wrong battle.
Poverty will continue to be a problem in this country
as long as our government allows businesses and corporations
to underpay their employees,
and as long as we live in a country where the
conditions undermine the lower class
by keeping them poor
while the rich get richer.
Greedy politicians and businessmen/women
are taking more than they need,
leaving their voters and employees sluggish
and making it almost impossible
to provide food, clothes, and shelter for their loved ones...

basic necessities of life
we can't afford
but they have so much that in five lifetimes they would still have
leftovers.

Think outside the box,
become open-minded
and realize everything is connected.
Without these,
you will not be ready to change
as you may think there is nothing to change.
Start with your body,
change the way you eat,
then change your mindset.
"United we stand,
divided we fall."
"Together an army of ants,
can overpower an elephant."

**Future**

What do you see for the future?  You don't want to know what I see.  I see more careless commercial and residential development and destruction of the Earth by those who wish to profit from our ignorance.  I see power and knowledge in the hands of few, as well as wealth, health, and wise living. My mind and heart ache when I see more pollution of the air, land, and water; (wasteful) development of former farm land; and unauthorized experimentation of our food.

These are just some of the things that I see...I see more but I will let you digest what has been said so you can make room for changes in your current mindset.  Soon, very soon, it will be too late to roll back the clock on the irreversible damage/destruction.  Change takes time, forethought and knowledge, as well as an envisioned goal.

You should grow your own food.  If you decide to shop, then buy certified organic produce from your local food cooperative or another natural foods store.  Consume and waste less.   Stop using toxic and poisonous cleaners/chemicals and replace them with natural, non-toxic, biodegradable, and multi-tasking products.  Seek out the remaining farms and plead with the owners to keep their land for-ever. Request your city/town to put a moratorium on the development of new neighborhoods/subdivisions until all current dwellings are occupied, including those that have been abandoned.

What is the reason for the continued ~~white flight~~ urban sprawl?

Pass this knowledge onto others because time is of the essence and the countdown for positive change has already begun.

## Rally to Blacks — New Year's Resolution

In this new year, let's make a resolution to quit patronizing and working for those businesses that are destroying our health; that unfairly treat their workers—no health insurance, forced and unpaid OT, climate of fear that keeps employees from speaking out or forming a union—here and abroad; that inject antibiotics into their livestock; that use artificial or synthetic ingredients in their products; that endorse and/or use GE (Genetically Engineered) or GMO (Genetically Modified Organisms) in the food that they grow, sell, package, and/or distribute.

We must support the grocers and food co-operatives that sell certified organic, heirloom, and all-natural food; restaurants that cook and prepare healthy, non-fried food, and offer vegetarian menu options; and companies that treat their employees with respect, dignity, offers them a living wage (or close to one), access to unions if needed, paid OT, and health insurance.  This means that we must arm ourselves with knowledge, so that we can become smarter consumers.

We must quit falling for propaganda given to us by the media and councils that have a bias (i.e., Dairy Farmers of America).

Last year, how many of us died before age 50 from preventable illnesses related to our health and lifestyles?  Does your boy/girl friend, significant other, fiancé, brother/sister, mother/father, aunt/uncle, cousin, neighbor, or friend have to be the next one to die from a preventable disease before we begin to make wiser choices?  If not, then what does it take?

We have to change our lifestyles and eating habits, so that we can see and spend time with our grandchildren and great-grandchildren.  In doing so, we must let our pockets do the talking...we must stop supporting businesses that are "killing us softly" through air, water, and land pollution; sell and produce GE/GMO food; inject chemicals or hormones into our food; and sell food that is detrimental to our health and well-being.

I have compiled a very short list of businesses that we should boycott forever, if we wish to change things for the better.

• **McDonald's**. They may sponsor good causes, but their food is fucking up our mental, emotional, and physical health every time that we consume it.

Online Resources:

"Super Size Me"
http://www.freedocumentaries.org/film.php?id=98

"Group tackles McDonalds over trans fat promise"
http://www.foodnavigator.com/Financial-Industry/Group-tackles-McDonalds-overtrans-fat promise

"Parents Advocating School Accountability Fast Food and Junk Food Information Page"
http://www.pasasf.org/nutrition/fastfood.html

"Fear of Frying"
http://www.alternet.org/envirohealth/19009/

"Chronic Conditions And Diet - Additives, Asthma, And Secondary Reactions"

http://www.eklhad.net/foods/foods6.html *[no longer available]*

• **All fast food** restaurants.  If you must eat out, go to a dine-in restaurant.  However, it is healthier to prepare and cook your own food, especially food that is fresh and organic.

• **Wal-Mart (aka Wally World)**.  There are few, if any happy employees working in their stores.  In 1999, it was the 2nd most sued company in the world.  And we have to remember that "cheap" prices come with a human cost.

Online Resources:

"UFCW | Wal-Martization and Wages"

http://www.ufcw.org/press_room/fact_sheets_and_backgrounder/walmart/wages.cfm *[no longer available]*

"2/16/2004 Press Release — New Report Details Wal-Mart's Labor Abuses and Hidden Costs"

http://edworkforce.house.gov/democrats/releases/rel21604.html *[no longer available]*

"Wal-Mart Litigation Project"

http://www.walmartlitigation.com/

"WAL-MART: The High Cost of Low Prices"

http://www.walmartmovie.com/

"Wal-Mart Watch"

http://walmartwatch.com/

"The Wal-Mart Effect | Charles Fishman"

http://www.walmarteffectbook.com/

"WakeUpWalMart.com"

http://makingchangeatwalmart.org/

"The Costs Of WalMartization Of America"

http://rense.com/general61/costo.htm

• **Nike**.  Over priced shoes come with a human cost.

Online Resources:

"Global Exchange : Nike Campaign"

http://www.globalexchange.org/fairtrade/sweatfree/nike

"Boycott Nike Home Page"

http://www.viet.net/web/nike//public_html/

"*Kasky v. Nike, Inc.*"

http://www.corpwatch.org/article.php?id=3448

"Nike Sweatshops - Unlocking the Power of Poverty"

http://www.toolness.com/nike/

• **Home Depot**.  Is Home Depot the "Wal-Mart" of home improvement stores?  If so, what can we consumers do about it?

Online Resources:

"Hometowns, Not Home Depot"

http://www.sprawlbusters.com/hometown.html

"Home Depot to Pay $5.5 Million to Resolve Class Discrimination Lawsuit in Colorado"

http://www.eeoc.gov/press/8-25-04.html

"Home Depot Class Action Lawsuit"

http://www.power-ofattorneys.com/PPF/page_ID/22/class_action_detail.asp *[no longer available]*

"Supreme Court won't hold back Home Depot suit"

http://www.lubbockonline.com/news/030497/supreme.htm

"No Depot"

http://www.nodepot.org/ *[no longer available]*

"No Home Depot Coalition – Northeast Los Angeles"
http://www.friendsofatwatervillage.org/nohomedepot.html

• **GE and biotechnology companies.** You are doing what to our food?! What effect will it have on me, my family, and others? We didn't ask for the genes of seeds to be altered! The top six companies are Monsanto, Syngenta AG, BASF, Bayer CropScience, Dow Agrosciences, and Pioneer Hi-Bred International.

Online Resources:

"GMO Food Labeled, But Not For Americans Press Release 10oct02"
http://www.mindfully.org/GE/GE4/Not-Labeled-For-Americans10oct02.htm

"GE Free Hits the Big Screen"
http://www.organicconsumers.org/ge/ge-free-movie.cfm

"Mounting Evidence of Genetic Pollution from GE Crop"
http://www.organicconsumers.org/ge/gepollution.cfm

"Soy Info Online!"

http://www.soyinfo.com/haz/gehaz.shtml

"The Campaign – Grassroots Political Action"

http://www.thecampaign.org/ *[no longer available]*

"Californians for GE–Free Agriculture"

http://www.calgefree.org/

"Major U.S. Companies Drop Genetically Engineered Foods in Europe"

http://www.lightparty.com/Health/CompaniesDropGEEurope.html

"Say no to genetic engineering | Greenpeace International"

http://www.greenpeace.org/international/en/campaigns/agriculture/problem/genetic-engineering/

"GENETICALLY ENGINEERED FOOD"

http://www.afrocentricnews.com/html/food.htm

"Biotechnology – Animals and Agriculture"

http://www.councilforresponsiblegenetics.org/Projects/PastProject.aspx?projectId=12#Articles

"genetically engineered foods"

http://www.netlink.de/gen/fa1gan.html#whatis *[no longer available]*

"Approval of GM Crops Illegal, US Federal Courts Rule"

http://www.i-sis.org.uk/Approval_of_GM_Crops_Illegal.php

"Sustainable Agriculture"

http://www.i-sis.org.uk/susag.php

"Food for Maine's Future: Genetically Engineered Crops on the Market"

http://www.gefreemaine.org/staticpages/index.php?page=20040812122617881 *[no longer available]*

"Genetic Roulette: The Gamble of Our Lives"

http://geneticroulettemovie.com/

• **Pharmaceutical companies** that sell drugs, which weaken the immune system (OTC/prescription allergy medicines), are addictive, and/or have side effects like death, stroke, heart attack, cancer, asthma, arthritis, breathing problems, etc.

Online Resources:

"RxList — The Internet Dug Index for prescription drugs and medications"
http://www.rxlist.com/drugs/alpha_a.htm

"JAMA — Abstract: Incidence of Adverse Drug Reactions in Hospitalized Patients: A Meta-analysis of Prospective Studies, April 15, 1998, Lazarou et al. 279 (15): 1"
http://jama.amaassn.org/cgi/content/abstract/279/15/1200

• **Tobacco (cigarette and cigar) and alcohol manufacturers**

# Action Items

21 February 2009

Yesterday I thought about changing how my book ends and it's purpose in the overall scheme of things. I decided that as part of my on-going effort to change the way that we collectively think, act, and live, it is **not** enough for me to create a(n) (e-)book. I needed to do more if I wanted to help foster positive changes. Therefore I created a "to do list" or list of action items that I would like for everyone that reads and/or purchases my (e-)book to implement.

1) Re-establish or create a garden. We must take matters into our own hands and become self-reliant. One method is resurrecting the art of growing food.

Gardens work on many different levels. Gardens help us to become more loving, nurturing, patient, and spiritual. It is good exercise; it can help build and strengthen relationships; and gardens will provide you, your family, and/or friends with fresh produce that can help one to become healthier. Gardening has a financial incentive as the price of food is increasing. It can also help alleviate and prevent dis-eases caused by factory farms and consuming GE/GMO "foods."

In 1999 or 2000, I started to realize that knowing how to grow food would become a life skill as I knew that there would be a time when low and middle income people would find it financially difficult to buy food, and sadly, this is beginning to happen.

About four years ago, I began gardening again. Since then, I have become healthier, more patient, and have re-connected with Nature, while developing a love for growing food and providing others with the knowledge and desire to garden.

2) Seek internal peace and then help to create lasting external peace.

3) Learn a foreign language and about the people that speak it.

4) Eat healthier, think healthier, and become healthier.

"Becoming a Healthier You"

http://ecoccs.com/BecomingHealthierYou_Resources.pdf

5) (Begin to) Think outside the box.

This page has been intentionally left blank.

# EPILOGUE

19 August 2012

   The poetry found within this book has been edited in minor ways as I wanted to keep its original intent and purpose intact. After I write a poem or while writing one, I allow my mind, body, and spirit to work as O.N.E. Sometimes I have a topic in mind but most of the time my mind is like a blank page as I write down the thoughts given to me by the Universe and its infinite wisdom.

   I cover diverse topics in my writing, especially my poetry. And even though some things may not seem related (today), if you read the book at a later time and date you may begin to see the hidden and visible connections.

   I am not a technology enthusiast, however, I do try and support entities that do good work, which is why this book has been created with Open Source Software. For more information on Open Source

127

Software, check out https://www.EConsultingllc.org/oss.

My e-book was created using OpenOffice.org.  I did my copy editing for this book using LibreOffice.  The book that you see today has been laid out using the desktop publisher Scribus.  And the cover has been designed with The GIMP.

Sincerely,

*Obiora Embry*

www.ingramcontent.com/pod-product-compliance
Lightning Source LLC
Chambersburg PA
CBHW080913020726
47502CB00008B/2448